Square Foot G
For begin

Table of Contents

Table of Contents 2

Introduction 3

Chapter 1: The Planning Stage 5

Chapter 2: Constructing your Garden 9

Chapter 3: Soil Preparations 16

Chapter 4: When, What and How to Plant? 24

Chapter 5: Going Organic 31

Introduction

Starting a home garden should be easy and fun. These two qualities make square-foot gardening appealing even to people who have never done gardening all their lives.

In many parts of the world, gardening is considered only as a hobby for people who are near their retirement age. It is not a hobby considered by people who are in their working age. The people behind square foot gardening have changed this perspective in many areas around the globe.

Anyone can do square foot gardening. You don't need a very wide backyard to do it. This is the problem of most people. They get discouraged from gardening because they think that their property lacks enough space for it. Square foot gardening takes care of that concern.

You also need very little resources to start this project. The amount of time, money and energy that you need to spend in this method is but a fraction of what you would spend in traditional gardening methods. Most of the prescribed materials are sustainable and easy to find. The structural materials used are also common in any part of the world. You may already have some of these materials lying around the house.

This book will guide you from day one to your first harvest. After that, all you have to do is to repeat the process with different types of plants. As you improve your square foot gardening techniques, the amount of your backyard produce will be enough to feed your whole family.

We hope that this book will convince you to be an avid gardener.

Want to receive our special bonus content? Make sure to sign up for Evelyn's mailing list: http://eepurl.com/VuaVX

Chapter 1: The Planning Stage

Planning your garden will ensure that you will not waste much of your resources on errors. It also improves your motivation because at the end of the planning stage, you will already have a mental picture of what your garden will look like.

Here are some factors that beginners should consider when planning their first square foot garden:

Start small if you only have a little gardening experience

If you have never done gardening before, then you should start with one box in your backyard. Pick a group of plants that you need in your home and start looking for seeds of those vegetables or flowers.

Planning a big project may frustrate you. Too much frustration will result to you abandoning it. Make sure that you have the time to tend to your garden every day. There will be some days where you only need to check your garden and there will be days where you will need to do some heavy lifting. Most of the work in square-foot gardening comes at the beginning. Be ready for that day by making sure that you don't have other scheduled affairs.

Consider the time that you can spend each day

Gardening can be an addictive hobby especially if you are good at it. You don't want to be late for work because you spent too much time in your garden. Set a gardening time each day. Square foot gardening will lessen the amount of work required to grow your crops and flowers. You only need to spend less than an hour each day on your square boxes.

Think of your overall budget for your gardening project

You don't need much to start you square foot gardening hobby. You will need pieces of wood that you can use as the walls of your boxes. If you have sources for these types of wood around your area, then you don't need to buy them. If you are located in a city where these types of wood are expensive, you could use bricks or cinder blocks that will get the job done. Aside from these, you will also need to prepare a budget for the soil that you will use.

You will also need to find the materials that will be used for the soil. The types of materials needed will be discussed in later chapters. You should call local nurseries to check the prices of these materials. You should also start planning about making your own home compost. You need to gather all plant-based biodegradable trash in your backyard. These materials are necessary to get good soil without the use of fertilizer.

Setting your Goals

The first part of planning is always setting your objectives. You need state what you want to achieve with your garden. You should decide whether you want to produce flowering plants or vegetables. Many people like doing a little bit of both.

If you plan on producing vegetables on a regular basis, then you should decide on the types that you want to produce and the amount that you need to harvest. You should also do a quick Google search on the length of time for these types of vegetables to become ready for harvesting. This will help your create a timeline for reaching your goals.

Picking the Right Location

The next step involves scouting for location. Take a walk around your property to look for a great area to place your square foot garden boxes. They should be near the house to make them easier to see. It is ideal if you pick locations that are visible from the places in the house where you usually hang out. Being able to see your garden reminds you of your gardening responsibilities. This motivates you to work. As a result, you will do a better job of consistently taking care of your plants.

It's also better to select a place that receives enough sunlight. Plants need around seven to nine hours of sunshine every day. Avoid areas near trees or bushes. The shade will prevent maximum growth of your plants. The seeds of some types of trees and bushes may also fall on your box and grow. Not all plants require the same amount of sunlight. If you have some shady areas, you could do some research on the type of local plants that grow well in shady areas.

It is also important to pick a place that allows water to drain when it rains. Excess water will cause the roots of many flowers and vegetables to rot. If your whole property does not drain well, you can elevate certain areas where you will place your boxes. You could also build a drainage system for the whole area.

Making a Plan on Paper

If you have chosen a place where you can start your square foot garden, you should create a plan on paper. Try to imagine what the area will look like when you are done developing it into a garden. Decide on the best location for flowering plants and vegetables.

If you already have the picture in your mind, draw the entire land area and the parts where the squares will go. The principle of square foot gardening also emphasizes on the pathway that you will use to walk around your garden. It is necessary that each box has a path around it. These paths allow you to see the whole box and all the plants that are in it. Blind spots are usually where diseases and pests begin to grow.

If your lot or the space that you have is not irregular in shape, you should line the boxes up in isles. You will be able to use space more efficiently if the boxes are arranged this way. If you are planting flowers or ornamental plants, you should base the boxes' locations on the overall design theme of your lot.

Planting on non-soil surfaces

The best part about square foot gardening is that you don't have to limit it to the backyard. You could build the boxes on wooden-floored patios or decks as long as these areas fit the criteria discussed in the earlier part of the chapter. These types of spaces usually have a smaller area compared to lots. You could build smaller boxes to adjust to the space available in your property. The prescribed size of boxes in this book is 4 x 4 feet. You could do 2 x4 or 2 x 2 feet variations if you have smaller spaces to work with.

Plan your watering and drainage system

You should also include the sources of water in your property when planning. If you use a garden hose, you should make sure that they are able to reach the location of your boxes. You should also consider installing a dripping system so that you no longer need to manually water your boxes.

If your property has the tendency to collect water during the rainy season, you should elevate the areas where you will put your garden boxes. You can do this by transferring soil from other areas of your property.

You should also allow the water to flow out of your property. You should build an exit path for the water to pass through to make sure that you will not have drainage problems during the rainy season.

Chapter 2: Constructing your Garden

Don't be intimidated by this chapter. A square foot garden is easy to construct using materials that can be easily obtained. The basic structure that you need to construct is a box that will hold the soil.

Square foot gardening uses this type of structure because it is more efficient in using space. They also look great in your backyard. Traditional gardening suggests to plant crops in the soil arranged in rows and columns. This arrangement works for large-scale farming but not for backyard planters. Boxes allow you to allot a small space in your backyard to a specific type of plant.

Crop Gardening Misconceptions

The reason why many people still use the old methods is because these methods are still taught in many gardening seminars. One of the traditional methods of planting suggests that all plants should be planted three feet apart. This method was developed based on the way farmers plant their crops. This method is inefficient in the use of both energy and space. If you use this method, you will not be able to maximize the space that you have in your backyard. Most of the space will be spent in paths in between crops.

Many crops don't need this much space to grow. Many of them can grow with only 6 inches of space in between crops. The types of crops that you can plant this way will be enumerated in later chapters.

Traditional gardening also teaches to plant the same type of crops that is right for the current season. This method is used in farms so that they can have enough produce during the planting season to feed their family for the whole year. Farmers only plant these types of crops because they sell well.

You do not need to follow this method. You could plant the variety of crops in your backyard depending on the needs of your family.

It is a common mistake to think that plants need their roots to grow deep downwards to be able to produce healthy fruits and leaves. Many types of crops grow well in soil only 6 inches deep. By providing the plants with enough nutrients and moisture that they need in upper part of the soil, the roots no longer need to go deep.

Constructing the boxes

The boxes suggested by square foot gardening are necessary to increase the efficiency of the use of space in your garden. It also improves the efficiency of your use of energy and time. In the old method of planting in rows and columns of the same plant, you need to water and fertilize the whole cultivated area to make sure that the roots will grow deep and wide. This method however, makes the land susceptible to weed growth. Weed seeds will grow in the watered and fertilized areas that do not have plants. People used to spend all day cutting the weeds in their garden. This process makes them hate gardening.

The square foot gardening system is designed for people who don't want to work that hard in gardening. We start with building the gardening boxes.

To build a gardening box, you will need four pieces of tough wood and 12 deck screws. These are the ideal materials to use but you can also use other materials depending on what are available to you.

If you are using lumber, the ideal thickness of the wood should be 2x6 inches. You should use rough lumber because they are thicker than those that have polished surfaces. They should be 4 feet in length. This is the ideal length for the average person to be able to reach the middle of the box from any angle without difficulty.

Here are more detailed instructions on how to do it:

1. Gather the lumber, the screw and the carpentry tools.
2. Cut the sides of the wood to achieve the suggested dimensions.
3. Arrange them by rotating the corners. You should end up with a square structure. Make sure that each side is of equal length.
4. If you are satisfied with the arrangement of the wood, use a drill and the deck screws to fasten the edges. They should be 4 inches long to make sure that they hold the wooden planks together.
5. Use 3 screws to fasten each side. This will be strong enough to hold the weight of the soil inside the box.

You could place weed cloth in the bottom of the box to prevent the weed seeds in the ground from creeping upwards. You could also use plywood to make a bottom for your box. This is necessary if you plan on moving the box around. Here are the instructions on attaching the plywood bottom to your box:

1. Cut the plywood to the same dimensions as your box.
2. Place the cut square plywood on top of the box.
3. Screw it in place using six evenly spaced screws in each side
4. Flip the box to reveal the hollow side.
5. Drill an abundant amount of holes in the plywood to allow the water to seep down.
6. Place the box in the desired position.

You now have your ideal box for your square foot gardening project. The next step is to place soil in it. Square foot gardening creator, Mel Bartholomew, has his own soil mix if it is available in your areas. However, you could also mix your own soil if you have no access to Mel's Mix. The process of mixing will be discussed in later chapters.

The next step is to place the grids. These grids will not only make your garden look neat but it will also help you organize your plants. The ideal material to be used for making grids is wood lath. They are sturdy and they don't easily cut like cloth or string. You should check if they are straight because some of the ones sold in stores are not cut well.

If you are located in the tropics, you could also use bamboo lath. These are inexpensive and they are water resistant.

To attach the grid in your box, follow these instructions:

1. Cut the lath into the right length (6 pieces of 4-foot wooden lath).

2. Measure the length of the sides of the box with a tape and make a mark with a pencil for every foot from the edges. If you do it right, there should be three marks in each side with 1-foot space in between each mark.

3. Position each lath so that each end is touching the mark you made on opposite sides of the square. The end result is 16 smaller boxes within your gardening box.

4. Make a whole in each end of the laths and screw them in place.

5. Reinforce the intersection of two laths by drilling a whole and putting a screw in them.

You now have a ready-to-use gardening box.

Building a protection for your garden

If you have animals around your yard, it's probably a good idea to create a protective covering for your square foot garden. One of the advantages of having a square-shaped box garden is that its regular shape makes it easy to cover. You can make a square shaped covering with a slightly larger area than the box. The type of material to use depends on the type of threat you are covering it from. If you are covering it from pets like cats or dogs, you can use chicken wire. On the other hand, if you want to protect it from insects, you may need to find nets with smaller holes.

To create this protective structure, you should follow these steps:

1. Collect the following materials:

    Four 1 x 2 inch pieces of lumber; they should be slightly more than four feet long.

    Chicken wire or net with smaller holes

    Screws or nails and plastic ties

2. Make a square structure with your lumber, similar to the shape of your gardening box. Adjust the length of the wood if they are too long by cutting.

3. Decide on the desired height of the structure by considering the maximum height of your plants when they become mature.

4. Cut the chicken wire to the desired length according the height that you need.

5. Bend the chicken wire at a 90-degree angle on each side to create a U-shaped structure.

6. Staple the two ends of the U-shaped chicken wire to the square wooden frame.

7. Cut additional chicken wire to cover the exposed sides.

8. You could use plastic ties to attach them to the other chicken wire and staples to attach them to the wooden frame.

Structural support for your plants

Some plants tend to bend when they grow too tall. This is a common concern among people who use the square foot gardening system because the box is only 6 inches deep. To prevent the plants from falling down when they grow tall, you should put a dome support over it.

Here's how you can do it:

1. Gather the following materials:

    2 10-foot PVC pipes that are ½ inch in diameter

    Plastic cable ties

2. Burry each end of one pipe on one corner of the box. It should touch the bottom of the box.

3. Bend it until it reaches the opposite edge of the box and secure that end too.

4. Do the same with the other two edges and the remaining pipe. The highest point of the bent pipes should touch.

5. Join the intersecting parts of the pipes together with a strong cable tie.

6. You can use various types of nets to protect your box.

Vertical support

If you plan to plant crops that make vines, you should prevent their vines from going out of the net by creating additional support over your box. You may need to use steel bars or pipes when constructing this type of support because the vines can become heavy. Wooden frames may not be strong enough to carry the vines when they become mature. Wooden frames also begin to become weak over time. As they are exposed to changing weather, their integrity weakens.

You only need to use metal for the frames. You could use chicken wire to add areas where the vines will cling to. You can add any type of net-like material if you no longer have any chicken wire available.

To make this work, you should plant crops with vines on the outer areas of your box. This way, they will have a shorter route to your vertical support.

Your garden structures are now ready.

Chapter 3: Soil Preparations

One of the revolutionary aspects of square foot gardening is the soil used in the project. In traditional gardening, most of the manual labor goes to the cultivation of the soil. To make it worst, there are areas where the soil is just not suitable for gardening.

You don't have to worry about this anymore. Just follow the instructions in creating Mel's Mix to create the perfect garden soil that will work with any type of plant.

Another advantage of using this mix is that you no longer need fertilizers. All the necessary nutrients needed by the plants can be found in the mix.

What do you need?

All you need to create Mel's Mix are garden compost, peat moss and vermiculite. You should mix an equal amount of each ingredient to fill the whole box.

Advantages of using this mixture

No weed seeds

The problem with using common soil is there are a lot of weed seeds in them. These weed seeds lie dormant until the soil provides them with the necessary conditions for growth. These include nutrients, moisture and the right temperature. Unfortunately, we provide them these conditions when we tend our soil every spring.

The ingredients used in Mel's Mix do not include common soil. Garden compost is a mixture of organic materials that are in the process of decomposition. This includes dead leaves and animal manure. The increase in temperature in the decomposition process will destroy much of the weed seeds that are mixed in.

The same is true with vermiculite. This is a mined type of rock, which is processed so that it will be able to hold moisture. Peat moss on the other hand, is a special type of decayed moss that is also excellent in holding moisture. Both of these materials don't contain weed seeds.

No more digging

One of the most difficult parts of gardening is digging. Clay, for instance, is very difficult to dig. The same is true with frozen soil. These types of soil make gardening impossible in certain locations or in certain parts of the year.

By using Mel's Mix, you will be able to plant even when the ground hasn't totally thawed yet. You could also plant even though the ground in your area is mostly made up of clay.

It holds just the right amount of water

In the past, gardeners are limited with the types of crops that they can plant depending on the water retention of the soil in their area. Most plants can't stand too much water in the soil. Their roots rot when the soil is always wet. Sandy soil on the other hand, is not good in retaining water. Only a few types of plants can grow in this type of soil.

Mel's Mix has peat moss, which is one of the best materials used for soil to improve water retention. The formula uses just the right amount of peat moss to prevent an increase in the soil's pH level. Vermiculite also retains just enough amount of water.

Both of these materials hold water well over a period of time but they do not become soggy or create a puddle. The excess water when it rains will drain down leaving just enough moisture needed by the plants.

You don't have to worry about the pH level of the ground

Many beginner gardeners are surprised by the amount of chemistry jargons used in many gardening books. One of the most common is pH, which is the measure of the level of acidity or alkalinity of a substance. Many plants don't want soil that is too alkaline or too acidic. You don't have to worry about this part because Mel's Mixture is at the optimum pH level for plant growth. If you follow the instructions properly, you will be able to plant anything in your soil.

The three components

Compost

Compost is a soil-like substance made up of decayed plant and animal waste. It is rich in minerals and nutrients needed by plants. Commercial compost is available in your local gardening and home shops.

Where to get it:

As mentioned above, you can buy compost from stores but that is not the best source. These types of compost are usually made up of one type of material. They are usually waste materials of industrial processes like saw dust. They are allowed to decay and mixed with a little bit of soil.

The square-foot gardening originator suggests that you make your own compost from home. Gather all the biodegradable plant-based wastes you have and put them in a composting bin. You should also include the trash from your garden maintenance like dead leaves and branches. You could also include manure from animals that consume plants.

There are two types of decomposition based on the presence of oxygen: aerobic and anaerobic decomposition. Aerobic decomposition happens when a decaying material is exposed to air. This is the preferred process when making compost because it allows biodegradable materials to decompose without the presence of too many harmful microorganisms. It also doesn't have the smell that we associate with rotten things.

If not done properly, some parts of your compost may undergo anaerobic decomposition. You don't want this to happen because the microbes that facilitate this type of decomposition are pathogenic to some types of plants. To be on the safe side, you should make sure that your compost will undergo aerobic decomposition.

Aerobic decomposition only happens when certain factors are present.

Aeration

As the name suggests, the material should be in the presence of oxygen. Anaerobic decomposition happens when you have a big pile of compost or when you bury it underground. When you have a big pile of compost for instance, the inner part of the pile will not have access to air. The existing bacteria in the pile will use up all the oxygen. When all of it is used up, the anaerobic bacteria will increase in number and take over the decomposition process.

To make sure that your pile will have enough aeration, you should make sure that it is mixed constantly. This will expose all the parts of your pile to oxygen making aerobic decomposition possible.

Enough moisture

The microbes responsible for aerobic decomposition also need enough water. Your pile should always be moist. However, you should not allow it to flood.

The right temperature

As the decomposition process happens, the temperature of your pile will increase. The heat is a wasted form of energy emitted from the process. You should prevent the pile from getting too warm. Making sure it's always moist will help decrease the temperature. Constantly mixing it will also prevent the temperature from rising in the inner parts of the pile.

Compost management

Cut everything into bite-sized pieces

Cutting them to little pieces will increase the surface area where the microorganisms can work on. Leaves and stems in particular are naturally resistant to microbes. You need to cut them to give the bacteria an entry point. This will hasten the process.

Mix the pile constantly

To allow the proper conditions to happen, you need to make sure that the pile is mixed and turned every now and then. As mentioned above, doing this will lessen the temperature in the inner part of the pile and provide oxygen to the less oxygenated parts.

Moisten the pile regularly

Don't expose the pile to too much sunlight because this will increase evaporation of moisture in the outer parts. Also make sure that it is located in an area with adequate drainage when it rains.

Add a variety of ingredients

Make sure that there are many types of ingredients in your pile. They will decay faster if there is a presence of manure and vegetable shaving in your kitchen. You could also add all the grass clippings from your yard. If there are larger pieces of leaves present, cut them into little pieces.

Vermiculite

This material is a special type of rock grounded up to small particles. It is mined all over the world for many purposes. They later undergo a heating process. The process increases the size of some of the particles. Their sizes vary from very fine particles to some as large as a pebble. A distinct characteristic of vermiculite is the presence of small cavities where roots can grow around. These cavities also hold a lot of water and prevent the soil from clumping and becoming compact. This type of soil condition will allow the roots to grow freely.

Vermiculite is not very popular among older gardeners because there were rumors that it contained asbestos. There are now brands that sell asbestos-free vermiculite. You should look for these brands in your local garden shops.

You may need to call a few gardening stores to find this material. Many stores still don't sell them. If you do find a store that does, you will have the option to buy fine, medium or coarse varieties. Choose the coarse variety because they are the best at keeping moisture.

Peat Moss

Peat moss is a type of sphagnum moss that grows dense in boggy areas. They are very absorbent and they tend to hold moisture for a very long time. Some people may say that this material is not sustainable. That's because it is only largely found in countries in the northern hemisphere. American peat moss mostly comes from areas like Canada where there are abundant supplies.

You will only need a small amount of peat moss in your garden. Each square-foot box only needs 1/3 peat moss and you no longer need to add more in the future.

There may be some countries where this material is not available. Tropical countries in particular may need to import peat moss from countries in the northern hemisphere. There are other sustainable alternatives to this material. The amount that you include in your mixture should be adjusted if you decide to change the material.

Mixing the right amount

To know how much of these materials to buy or collect, you should first calculate the volume that you need for your gardening box. A 4 x 4 feet box that is 1 foot deep requires sixteen cubic feet of soil. If you use the prescribed 6-inch deep box, you will only need half that amount which is 8 cubic feet of Mel's Mix.

You should then divide the total by three and that's the volume you need to buy for each material if you had one box. If you have multiple boxes, you will need to multiply that amount by the number of boxes.

There are various ways that you can easily create Mel's Mix. If you have space wide enough, you can just put each ingredient in a concrete surface and mix it with a shovel. However, dry vermiculite and peat moss can be dusty and some small particles may float in the air. You should make sure to use paint mask while mixing to avoid triggering some allergic reactions.

A better way of mixing is using a wide unused tarpaulin. Put all the ingredients in the middle of the tarp. You should then spread the materials evenly in the surface using a shovel or a rake. Fold the tarp to mix the ingredients around. You should then spread them evenly and fold the tarp again to mix it all up. Repeat the process until you are satisfied with the mixture.

Do this process when there is no wind and it is not raining. It is easier to mix dry materials evenly but wind may blow them all over the place. Making it a little moist by spraying it with a mist of water will decrease the amount of dust if you are working on a windy day. Be careful not to add too much water because the materials will become too heavy to mix.

A third option is to use a wheel burrow to mix the soil. This is the best option when you are only mixing a small amount. Put the prescribed amount of each ingredient on the wheel burrow and mix it using a shovel or a garden spade. You should also use a small amount of water if the mixing process produces too much dust in the air.

If you have multiple boxes, you should buy the materials in bulk and mix them together all at once. Just store the excess in a safe dry place for future use when you decide to expand your garden.

After mixing the materials, you should spread them evenly in your box before placing the grids. Make sure that the soil is distributed evenly in the corners and the edges of the box. After adding the soil to your box, sprinkle it with water. This will prevent the wind from blowing the surface soil.

You should also check if the water drains properly in your box. If it creates a puddle, you may need to add holes in your plywood bottom or control the amount of water used when watering the plants. If everything is turning out nicely, you are now ready for planting.

Chapter 4: When, What and How to Plant?

Planting is the most exciting part of gardening. Growing a plant from seed is a very rewarding experience. Picking your harvest and using them in your kitchen will make you feel proud of your hard work.

What to plant

The usual process of backyard gardening is to plant as much as you can in a seedbed and transfer the ones that grow to the ground. Just like the other aspects of traditional gardening, this process is inefficient. The competition of growth between seeds in a seedbed will affect their initial growth. Many of the seeds will be overwhelmed by the other seeds.

Square-foot gardening promotes efficiency even in the use of seeds. The seeds that you don't plant today can be used in the future. To make sure that none of your seeds go to waste, you should set your gardening goals. Start by identifying the types of vegetables or root crops that you usually use. These are the most useful plants for you and these are the types that you should plant first.

You should also think of what you are going to do with your harvest. Are you going to sell them or are you going to use them at home?

If you have a way of selling them, then you can plant one type of crop in your gardening box. If you plan on using all your produce at home, then you should plant a variety of vegetables that you usually use in your kitchen.

When you become an experienced square-foot gardener, you can begin experimenting with vegetables and root crops that you haven't tried yet.

How much to plant

After deciding on the vegetables, root crops, or flowering plants that you want, you should visualize how they will fit in your gardening box. You should classify these plants according to their sizes. Vegetables like cabbages and broccoli are large types. Only one plant of these types will fit in each small square in your gardening box. Lettuces on the other hand, are medium sized vegetables and you can fit up to four of them in one square foot.

Smaller vegetables like bush beans and spinach are small and you will be able to fit nine vegetables of this size in one square foot. You will be able to fit sixteen of the smallest types of root crops like carrots, radishes and onions. Imagine the size of the root crops and vegetables that you want to plant and decide on the number of plants you will plant in each square foot based on their size.

Your gridlines will guide you in positioning your vegetables. You can even plant multiple types of vegetables in your gardening box. Varying the types of crops will prevent overplanting of one type of vegetable. You should also try to plan the crop rotation that you will use each year. Changing the types of plants in your garden regularly will control the population of specific pests in your garden. Pests tend to like specific types of plants.

A caterpillar in your cabbage plant for example, will only eat cabbage leaves. By changing the types of plants in your garden, you are preventing the reproduction cycle of one kind of pest. This will result to healthier plants with no need for insecticides.

How to plant

First, you need to gather the seeds of the plants that you want. They are usually available in agriculture shops and local nurseries. If you have them, the next step is to divide your one-foot square into smaller squares. The number of smaller square that you need depends on the size of the crop that you will plant.

For cabbage sized plants

If you are planting very large plants like cabbages, you can just make a hole in the middle of the one-foot square and put the seeds in each hole.

For lettuce sized plants

If four plants can fit in one square, you can draw a set intersecting line in each square. The two intersecting lines will produce four squares. Just make four holes in the middle of the smaller squares formed and put the seeds in each hole.

For spinach sized plants

To fit nine plants in one square, draw two evenly spaced horizontal lines and vertical lines within the one-foot square. The end result is nine smaller squares within the one-foot square. You can then make a whole with your finger in the middle of each smaller square and put the seeds in each hole.

For small root crops like onions

For the smallest root crops, you can divide the one-foot square into four smaller squares. You should then use your index and middle finger to make two pairs of holes in each square. You can then put the seeds in these holes.

When putting the seeds, you should make sure to follow the prescribed depth of each plant. You can find this information in the labels of commercial seeds. If you did not buy your seeds, you could do a quick research on it online.

When watering these seeds, you should make sure that you use watering can or a hose nozzle that will make the water fall gently. The water should not disturb the deeper level of the ground where the seeds are located.

You also don't need to put too much water in the box. Because the soil is enclosed in a box, the moisture from the previous day will still remain in the soil the following day.

If you are planting young plants, you should be careful not to damage the roots. Follow the same process suggested above for planting seeds and mark the area where you will place them. Place them in the right position and put just enough soil to cover the roots and to keep the plant standing. Next, you should gently water them.

To properly plot the types of crops that you will plant in a particular part of the year, you should make a chart of the cycle of plants that grow in your area. Plants grow best when they are planted in the right season. You should learn what types of plants grow best in your area during summer, fall and spring.

You can follow this cycle to make sure that you will have healthy plants. You should particularly take note of the cycle of your favorite fruits, vegetables and root crops. Make a list of the foods that your children like and add them to your chart. You should also take note of the seasons when they grow best. Not planting them at the right season will affect their growth and the size of their fruits.

If you plan on selling your produce, you should do some research on the types of crops that sell fast. You should also consider crops that sell for higher prices. Visit your local vegetables sources and ask them of the crops that have low supply but are always sought-after by buyers. You should be able to make a good choice if you consider these factors

By planning your crop cycle in a chart, you will be able to prepare for the most unforgiving part of the year; fall. Forget winter; you will not be able to plant through that season. The best that you can do is to make the most out of your garden by growing plants through fall.

Planting through fall:

The first thing that you need to do is to pick the plants that are strong enough to survive this part of the year. There are vegetables that thrive in the cool climate of fall like broccoli and Brussels sprout. You could also plant root crops like carrots and radishes. Other leafy vegetables that do well in this season are lettuce, cabbage and spinach. You should research on the growing period of these vegetables to make sure that you will be able to harvest them before winter.

Most of these vegetables should be planted in the early parts of August. This will give them the necessary time to grow. There are some plants though, that can be planted later. These are the plants with shorter maturity time like spinach and lettuce.

You want to harvest these crops before the frost but there are root crops that taste better when harvested in the early parts of winter.

Plant care guidelines:

Deal with weeds as soon as you see them

Weeds are usually not a problem with square-foot gardening but there are times when weed seeds accidentally reach your soil mix. You should check your box every day for signs of weeds. You should pick them early to make sure that they don't have the chance to reproduce. You should also make sure that you remove all its parts including the roots. Some types of plants reproduce through their root system.

Never step on the soil

The box will prevent you from accidentally stepping on your plants. Your box should never be stepped on. Its dimensions will allow you to reach any area without difficulty. You should also give this instruction to the people who are helping you out with your garden.

Keep an eye out for plant diseases

There is always a chance that your plants will get sick. The microorganisms that cause these diseases are brought by insects or can be carried by the wind. You should do some research on the types of diseases that are common in your plants. You should check your plants every day for telltale signs of these diseases. If the particular disease affects just a small area, you should consider cutting it. There are some diseases that can be treated with natural remedies but if a large part of your plant is affected, you best action is to prevent it from spreading to other plants.

Avoid drowning your plants

It is also common for some gardeners to put too much water on their plants. As mentioned in previous chapters, this is not good for the roots of your plants. Root crops in particular rot fast if there is too much moisture in the soil. Their roots become soft and become susceptible to bacterial attacks.

Plant just enough crops to meet your goals

One of the advantages of dividing your gardening box into grids is that you can plant different varieties of vegetables in each grid box. Even if you only have one box, you can plant a variety of plants that will provide you with produce from spring until the early parts of winter. Remind yourself of your gardening goals and plant the right vegetables and fruits.

You can pick just enough according to your current needs

One of the advantages of having vegetables in the backyard is that you can pick only the amount that you need. If you need lettuce for a salad for instance, you can pick just enough leaves for your needs. When buying this type of vegetables, we are usually forced to buy a large amount according to the packaging of the stores. A large quantity of the vegetables that we buy, end up in the garbage. If you have a vegetable garden in your backyard, you will not be so wasteful.

Add some flowers to your vegetable garden

Even though you don't like flowers, you should consider adding them in one of your boxes. They attract pollinators that will also be beneficial to vegetables that bear fruits. Butterflies and bees are attracted to places that have a lot of blooming flowers. Adding these types of plants to your square-foot garden will increase the probability that your flowers will become fertilized and bear fruits.

They also attract predators that will take care of your pests. When you see a spider in your garden, let them be. They are there to deal with the unwanted caterpillars and insects.

Consider pruning the right plants

Crops that bear fruits like tomatoes usually need some pruning to make sure that all the energy of the plant goes to one direction. The theory suggests that by doing this, the fruits of these types of plants will become bigger and the stems will become healthier. This will also allow them to grow taller. This will take the fruits out of the reach of pests that come from the soil.

Pruning will also protect the plants with localized diseases. Cutting off parts that are infected will prevent the disease from spreading to the other parts of the plants and to other plants of the same type. Spotting these diseases early is crucial to prevent them from spreading.

Chapter 5: Going Organic

Organic gardening is a gardening approach of using beneficial scientific and traditional methods to yield safe-to-eat land produce. Though most of the practices of organic gardening are based on traditional planting, we could further enhance it by integrating it with the square-foot gardening program.

The agriculture industry has produced many types of chemical products that make farm and garden management easier. Some of these products however, stay on the crops that we grow even after washing them. Some of these chemicals that are toxic to the pests are also toxic to humans. Many have chronic effects to people's health.

Organic gardening promotes natural methods of dealing with pests. By doing organic gardening, you can literally pick the fruits of your labor and eat them on the spot.

It not only promotes people's health but also sustainable living. The practices in making the soil fertile, the choice of crops to be planted, and the resources used in farming and gardening should all have no harmful effects to the environment. The materials used in particular should be easily attainable and replaceable. Non-biodegradable materials can only be used if they are not thrown to the landfill immediately after use. They should be recycled continuously to make sure that they do not contribute to the garbage problem in an area.

Organic gardeners also avoid using foreign species of plants. These plants, if not controlled properly, may become invasive species. They may bring with them plant pathogens that local plants don't have immunity to. Some aggressively growing varieties may also compete with local plants for space, nutrients and moisture. The threats that these foreign species of plants bring may cause extinction of local plants.

Organic gardening also promotes the use of natural ways to deal with insect pests and plant diseases. For instance, organic gardeners make a habit of growing plants that attract beneficial insects to the garden. This is one of the natural defenses against pests. Instead of using insect killing chemicals that kill insects indiscriminately and also harm humans who ingest them, organic gardeners let natures' killers deal with them.

The practice of crop rotation throughout the year will also prevent the increase of the number of pathogens to a particular plant. Gardeners who plant the same types of crops and flowers all year long usually have problems with plant diseases. These pathogens are microorganisms that cause diseases in plants. In minor cases, they may cause discoloration in the leaves and the stems of the plants. They could also be very severe; spreading throughout your garden and killing all plants of the same breed.

Using organic approach to square-foot gardening

The entire square-foot gardening program is based on organic gardening principles. It uses natural sustainable materials in the soil mixture and it discourages the use of fertilizers of any kind. It also encourages planting of multiple types of plants.

Aside from the already discussed principles however, there are still some added practices that you need to learn to be able to create an organic square-foot garden.

You should have a habit of continuous self-learning

Organic gardening uses both traditional and modern approaches to gardening to obtain favorable results. Square-foot gardening's originator; Mel Bartholomew, never stopped questioning the existing practices of gardening back in the 70's. That was the reason why we have this easy gardening system today.

You should also adapt the same learning attitude when you start your organic square-foot garden. You should keep looking and reading for innovative ideas that you can add to your garden to make it more sustainable and safe for both humans and the environment.

You should always use safe and natural means of solving garden problems

Much of the difficult parts of gardening are already addressed by the square-foot gardening system. You no longer have to worry about the hard work that is usually associated with gardening. You also don't need to worry about buying products like fertilizers to keep your ground fertile.

However, there will always be some unexpected concerns that are unique to your situation. One example is when pests attack your crops. Most gardeners would take the easy way out and buy the strongest insecticides that they could find. As a practitioner of organic gardening, you should look into the solutions of traditional gardeners in the past when dealing with these types of concerns. If there are no published organic solutions to these concerns, you should look into what new authors say about it.

If you already have a square-foot garden and you want to convert it to become organic, you should follow these steps:

Create a Yearly Crop Cycle Chart

This chart is similar to the one mentioned in the previous chapter. It contains that best crops for you to plant in a particular part of the year. The change that you need to make is in your choice of plants. You need to use the principle of companion planting. When planting tomatoes in your box for example, you could also add marigolds in an alternate square-foot. Many gardeners believe that marigolds repel damaging insects like aphids.

You should also avoid using foreign plants in your garden. These plants have long-term effects in the environment that can be harmful to local plants.

Practice seed saving

When your plants grow, you should make sure that you save seeds from the healthiest plants. Keep them in a safe place and be aware of their shelf life. Labeling them will help you identify them in the future. Seed saving will help make your garden sustainable. It will also save you some money in the future because you no longer need to buy new sets of seeds from local nurseries.

Introduce plants that will become habitats of beneficial insects

As mentioned above, using insecticides will kill all insects in your garden indiscriminately. To deal with pests that may affect your crops, you need to introduce plants that will attract predators for those pests. For instance, you should add flowering plants around your square foot garden to attract ladybugs and lacewings. These insects are predators to soft-bodied pests like caterpillars and aphids. They are also attracted to pollens making them minor pollinators in your garden.

Letting some insects live

You should not be alarmed when you see that your lemon tree has some caterpillars in them. Most gardeners would spray them with insecticides as soon as they see them. Organic gardeners allow some caterpillars to grow because they turn into butterflies and become pollinators. You should learn more about the insects in your garden to determine which ones will become beneficial in the future. The presence of these types of insects will also attract predatory creatures like spiders that will eat anything they can wrap in their web.

Handpicking pests

If you see pests that will never become beneficial to your garden, you should deal with them before they reproduce. Use your fingers on insects that are safe to pick by hand. You can put them in soapy water to instantly kill them without the use of pesticides.

Make your irrigation system efficient

Don't use automatic sprinklers in your garden because they are only meant for lawns. Most of the water that they spit will go to the paths or the leaves of the plants. Use a more efficient way of watering your garden boxes.

You could install an automated drip system instead of a sprinkler. These systems use very little water that go straight to the soil of your plants. There are various types of drip systems that you can use in different parts of your garden. You can put a commercial drip system tip for each plant in your garden box. Make sure that each plant gets its fair share of water.

Use local resources

If you are planning on making more garden boxes, you should use sustainable resources in your area. If lumber is too expensive for your budget for example, you can use other sturdy alternatives like bamboo or used wood. Work with what you have and make sure that they are sustainable. Avoid using non-biodegradable materials.

If products like peat moss are not available in your area, you could use a local alternative. This is a problem particularly in tropical areas in the dry seasons. If this a concern for you, find alternative sustainable materials that will help keep water in the soil. Many gardeners for instance use rice husk and coconut coir as alternatives.

Conclusion

Square-foot gardening was created to promote food production in your own backyard. With the knowledge you got from this book, you are ready to build your very first gardening box. You should not be afraid to start. Just follow the tips provided in this book and you will have a thriving set of crops in less than a month.

Though this book provided you with comprehensive information about square-foot gardening, you should continue to learn new principles that will improve your gardening skill-set.

Want to receive our special bonus content? Make sure to sign up for Evelyn's mailing list: http://eepurl.com/VuaVX

Why not check out Evelyn's other books?

Vegetable gardening for beginners
https://www.amazon.com/dp/B00K4YAA5M

Canning and preserving for beginners
http://www.amazon.com/dp/B00KXAQE4I

Cleaning your house: How to clean your house easy, fast and get organized
http://www.amazon.com/dp/B00JZ6VRMA

Printed in Great Britain
by Amazon